HOW TO PLAY LIKE A PRO

BASEBALL SKILLS

BY DAVE McMAHON

Enslow Publishers, Inc.
40 Industrial Road
Box 398
Berkeley Heights, NJ 07922
USA

http://www.enslow.com

Enslow Elementary, an imprint of Enslow Publishers, Inc.

Enslow Elementary® is a registered trademark of Enslow Publishers, Inc.

Library of Congress Cataloging-in-Publication Data
McMahon, Dave.
  Baseball skills : how to play like a pro / by Dave McMahon.
      p. cm. — (How to play like a pro)
  Summary: "Readers will learn how to hit, field, and many other
baseball skills"—Provided by pubisher.
  Includes bibliographical references and index.
  ISBN-13: 978-0-7660-3204-0
  1. Baseball—Juvenile literature. I. Title.
  GV867.5.M42 2009
  796.357092—dc22
  [B]

                                              2007048515

Credits
Editorial Direction: Red Line Editorial, Inc.
Cover & interior design: Becky Daum
Editor: Bob Temple
Special to thanks to Frank White, Minnesota Twins RBI League Coordinator and founder of Respect
Sports, for his help with this book.

Printed in the United States of America

10 9 8 7 6 5 4 3 2

To Our Readers: We have done our best to make sure all Internet Addresses in this book were active and appropriate when we went to press. However, the author and the publisher have no control over and assume no liability for the material available on those Internet sites or on other Web sites they may link to. Any comments or suggestions can be sent by e-mail to comments@enslow.com or to the address on the back cover.

♻ Enslow Publishers, Inc. is committed to printing our books on recycled paper. The paper in every book contains 10% to 30% post-consumer waste (PCW). The cover board on the outside of each book contains 100% PCW. Our goal is to do our part to help young people and the environment too!

Photo credits: AP Photo/Gene J. Puskar, 1, 19, 38; iStockPhoto/Ben Conlan, 4; iStockPhoto/Rob Friedman, 5, 20; AP/Denis Poroy, 7; iStockPhoto/Dave Herriman, 8; AP Photo, 9; iStockPhoto/Eliza Snow, 10; AP/Jeff Roberson, 11; iStockPhoto/Iris Nieves, 12; AP Photo/Mark Duncan, 13; AP/Ted S. Warren, 14, 22; iStockPhoto/Doug Webb, 15, 32; AP Photo/Nati Harnik, 17; AP Photo/Elise Amendola, 18, 25; AP/LM Otero, 21; iStockPhoto/Diane Diederich, 23; iStockPhoto/Michael Ciu, 24, 41; AP/Charlie Riedel, 27; AP/Keith Srakocic, 28; AP Photo/Carolyn Kaster, 29; iStockPhoto/Brent Reeves, 30; AP Photo/Al Behrman, 31; AP/Kathy Willens, 33; iStockPhoto/Donald Linscott, 34; AP/Dick Whipple, 35; AP Photo/Chris Pizzello, 37; AP Photo/Francis Specker, 39; AP Photo/James A. Finley, 40; iStockPhoto/James Boulette, 42; AP Photo/Stephen J. Carrera, 43; AP/Branimir Kvartuc, 44-45.

Cover Photo: AP Photo/Gene J. Puskar (large image); AP Photo/Elise Amendola (small image).

CONTENTS

BASEBALL PREGAME

Baseball players enjoy the sport because there are so many different athletic abilities that are required. Players must be able to hit, throw, catch, and run. But even if a player can do all these things, there's always room for improvement. Baseball players don't become great overnight. Years of practice are needed to learn the different aspects of the game.

Baseball is a team game. After all, what player would want to play all by himself? So find a friend, or get a group together,

and work on your game with some of the tips and drills provided in this book.

Don't forget that no matter how many times you miss when you are batting, or if you drop a fly ball, even the pros do the same thing.

Also, remember that sportsmanship and team-work are critical parts of what makes baseball a great game. So make sure to encourage your friends and teammates.

Right Fielder

Center Fielder

Second Baseman

First Baseman

Left Fielder

Shortstop

Pitcher

Third Baseman

Catcher

To learn more about the
basic rules of baseball, see
the resources listed on p.47!

HITTING

Players work on their hitting technique every day during the season. Professional teams have coaches to teach players how to hit. Hitting a pitched baseball is one of the most difficult things an athlete can do. After all, batters are considered successful if they get a hit three times out of ten.

Hitting a baseball requires good hand-eye coordination. The best way to become a better hitter is practice. The more good swings you can take, the more natural your swing will become.

If you're hitting, always wear a batting helmet.

Practice

Hitting off a tee is an easy way to develop your swing. Be sure to swing down slightly on the ball. A swing that goes up at the ball will create an easy pop fly for one of the fielders to catch.

Use different heights of the tee to get comfortable with pitch locations. Former New York Yankees star Don Mattingly often hit off a tee for two hours a day!

Keep your eye on the ball from the instant you see it leave the pitcher's hand. Watch the ball until the bat makes contact with it.

Batting Average

To find your batting average, divide the number of hits by the number of at-bats. For instance, if you had 30 hits divided by 100 at-bats, your average would be .300.

Ryan Howard (6) of the Philadelphia Phillies hit 47 home runs and drove in 136 runs in 2007. He ranked second in Major League Baseball in both categories.

CHOOSING A BAT

How tall are you? What level of baseball will you be playing? How much money will you be able to spend on a bat? What feels most comfortable to you? Those are among the questions to consider when choosing a bat.

Most youth baseball leagues in the United States favor aluminum bats. Aluminum bats are lighter than wood bats and allow the hitter to make a quicker swing.

As a batter, you want to generate as much power as you can when the bat connects with the ball. The quick swing of the aluminum bat provides more power when the bat connects with the ball. Also, wood bats break much easier. That can add up to quite an expense throughout a season for players who play a lot. Lighter bats are better for younger players.

How Old Are You?

Your age can help you find the right bat.

Age	Bat Length
5–7	24"–26"
8–9	26"–28"
10–11	28"–30"
11–12	30"–32"
13–14	31"–32"
15–16	32"–33"
17+	34"

Bats for Mom

Several Major League players used pink bats on Mother's Day in 2007. The bats were auctioned after the games to raise money for the Susan G. Komen Breast Cancer Foundation.

Wood Only

Not all states allow aluminum bats at the high school level. In North Dakota, high school baseball teams are required to play with wood bats only. Wood bats are generally safer, because the ball doesn't come off the bat at fielders as fast. Pro teams use wood bats.

Bobby Thomson chose the right bat the day he hit "The Shot Heard Round the World." His home run put the New York Giants in the 1951 World Series. It is one of the most famous home runs in baseball history.

STANCE

The first step in getting a hit is to find a comfortable stance at the plate. Your feet should be six to eight inches wider apart than your shoulders. Your weight should be more on your back foot than your front foot. Stand on the balls of your feet with your knees and hips bent.

Where you stand within the batter's box is up to you. Some players like to be even with home plate. Others stand closer to the pitcher, or farther back.

Stay Balanced

Comfort plays a big role in determining which stance to use. Try different types of stances. Move your front foot out a few inches to see if it feels better. Angle the front foot toward the pitcher slightly. Balance is very important.

HITTING

Bat is held back

Head is steady

Getting a Hit

After you hit the ball, run to first base. If the ball is caught in the air, or if the fielders can get the ball to first base before you touch the base, you are "out." If your ball hits the ground and you make it to first base before the fielders get the ball there, you are "safe." That's also called a "base hit."

Weight on back leg

Knees are bent

Power at the Plate

Albert Pujols broke into the major leagues in 2001 and quickly became one of the game's best hitters. He was named National League Most Valuable Player in 2005.

One easy approach to the swing involves four key elements: ready, load, squish, and follow through.

Ready: Hands are in front of the body at armpit height and the bat is resting on the shoulder.

Load: Shift the weight to the back foot, which will pull the front heel slightly off the ground.

Squish: The batter squishes the back foot as if squishing a bug with his or her toes. The weight stays on the back foot, but the body starts to shift forward as the hands start to move.

Follow Through: The momentum of the explosion between the bat and ball will take the bat into the follow through.

Knuckles

Hold the bat with the "knocking knuckles" from both hands in a straight line. The "knocking knuckles" are the knuckles used to knock on a door. This will strengthen the wrists.

Track It

As the pitcher begins the delivery, focus on the pitcher's window. This is the spot where the ball will actually leave the pitcher's hand. Don't look at the pitcher's body. Instead, focus on the window. Continue to focus on the ball at the point of contact with the bat. Keep the head down until the follow through is completed.

Head remains steady

Follow through with the swing

Front arm is extended

The 2007 season was a big one for Alex Rodriguez of the New York Yankees. He reached 500 home runs for his career and won his fourth American League MVP award.

Use the hips to provide extra power

Bunting for a Hit

Ichiro Suzuki of the Seattle Mariners is one of the best bunters in the major leagues. He bunts to try to get on base by getting out of the batter's box quickly. He actually starts his motion to first base while he is bunting.

Lower hand on the bat handle

Body turned slightly toward the pitcher, but not all the way

Upper hand near the fat part of the barrel

Squeeze Play

On a squeeze play, the batter bunts to try to advance a base runner from third base to home plate.

If the batter misses the ball on the bunt attempt, the catcher will most likely tag out the runner at home plate. Because of the varying degrees of success, it's one of the most exciting plays in baseball.

HITTING

BUNTING

Bunting is one of the most overlooked skills in baseball. A good bunter is a great asset to the team. A bunt can be used either to advance a runner or to get a base hit.

Moving up in the batter's box, closer to the pitcher, will help the batter bunt the ball into fair territory. Square the body toward the pitcher by pivoting so both feet point toward the field. Do not turn so much that the whole body is facing the pitcher. Facing the pitcher makes it very hard to get out of the way if the ball is pitched toward the batter.

Keep the lower hand on the bat handle. Slide the upper hand up the bat to the point where the bat head starts to get fatter. As the pitch arrives, handle the bat as if trying to "catch" the ball with the barrel. This will cushion the pitch and allow the bunt to drop more softly down to the ground.

Why bunt?

Dropping a bunt down one of the baselines is a way to get to first base safely. Another reason to bunt is to "sacrifice." This means to make an out on purpose to help a teammate get to the next base.

PITCHING

How important is a team's pitcher? He or she is usually the most important player on the team. There's no other player who can impact the outcome of a game as much as a pitcher can. Young players who learn the proper throwing motion should use that same motion as they learn how to pitch.

The focus should always be on throwing the ball across the plate, not on the speed or movement of pitches. If a pitch does not cross the plate, and the batter doesn't swing, it will be called a ball. If a batter gets four balls, he goes to first base.

Pitching the ball over the plate makes it easier for a pitcher to get outs.

Across Seams

From a fielding position, the ball should be thrown with two fingers across the seams. That makes the throw longer and straighter.

Try throwing the ball with two fingers lined up with, or on top of, the seams. This makes the ball curve easier, fall sooner, and harder for the batter to hit.

Throwing curveballs or other special pitches can be hard on a young person's arm. To keep from getting hurt, pitchers should not

Point Glove at Target

The glove should be pointed at the target with the arm comfortably bent. As the lead foot hits the ground, the ball is released. The glove then moves to the hip, with the thumb of the glove pointing up.

Johan Santana of the New York Mets won the American League Cy Young Award in 2004 and 2006 as the league's best pitcher. In his first eight seasons in the major leagues with the Minnesota Twins, he had 1,381 strikeouts.

DELIVERY

The delivery you should use when you pitch is determined by whether there are runners on base.

Generally, if there are no runners on base, you should pitch from the wind-up position. If there are runners on base, you should pitch from the stretch. The stretch is a quicker delivery, which makes it harder for a runner to steal a base.

In the wind-up position, the pitcher stands on the pitching rubber with both feet pointing toward home plate. The feet should be about six to twelve inches apart. The heels should be on the pitching rubber, with the front half of the foot hanging off the rubber.

In the stretch position, the pitcher begins with his feet pointing to one side, instead of to home plate. With the back foot on the rubber, the pitcher's weight is shifted to his back leg.

Practice

Learn to grip the ball by throwing it up into the air and catching it with your glove. Use the throwing hand to reach in for the ball and find the proper grip.

Prior to the pitch, the bare hand will be holding the ball inside the glove. Keep the back of the glove facing the batter and close to the chest so that no one can see the grip on the ball.

The Little League World Series is held every year in Williamsport, Pennsylvania. The best 12-year-old baseball teams from around the world compete for the championship.

19

FIELDING

A pitcher's reaction time is important because the pitcher makes split-second decisions after the ball is hit.

Pitchers should be ready to scoop up any ball that a batter hits near the pitcher's mound. Sometimes the ball is hit so fast off the bat that the pitcher relies on quick reflexes and instincts to make the catch. If a ball is tapped in front of the plate, the pitcher has to run fast to get it.

Practice

Have a player in the batter's box slowly roll a ball a few feet inside the first base line. From the pitcher's mound, see how quickly you can pick up the ball and make a throw to a player at first base.

Cover First

The pitcher's main priority on any ground ball hit to the right side of the infield is to cover first base.

Don't Hit the Runner

The pitcher needs to be able to make throws at a variety of speeds and angles. If the pitcher picks up a bunted ball down the first-base line, it's important to throw the ball a few feet to the inside of the first baseman. Otherwise, a straight throw could hit the base runner and allow him to reach base safely.

Keep the back toward first base

Use the bare hand to cover the ball as it goes into the glove

Bend the knee

Keep the glove open and let it act as a cushion for the ball

Keep the pivot foot stable

43

Daisuke Matsuzaka (right) came to the major leagues after having an exceptional career in Japan. He noted after his debut that the American baseball is a little bit harder to grip because it is bigger than the baseballs used in Japan.

The eight major pitches are the four-seam fastball, two-seam fastball, changeup, curveball, slider, split-finger, screwball, and knuckleball.

Old Enough

The recommended age for learning to throw a fastball is between 6 and 10 years old. The average speed for a fastball at the major-league level is 85 to 87 miles per hour.

PITCHING

FASTBALL

The first type of pitch that a young player should learn to throw is the fastball. There are two types of fastball grips: four-seam and two-seam. Regardless of what kind of pitch is thrown, the pitcher should always make sure to have a comfortable release.

For a two-seam fastball, place the index and middle fingers across the narrowest area of the seams. The thumb remains underneath, perpendicular to the seams. On this pitch, the batter sees two parallel seams in the rotation. Move the fingers across the widest part of the seam to throw a four-seamer.

The four-seam fastball is used to get the pitch up in the strike zone and is the easiest to locate (it can be thrown easily to any target). The two-seam fastball, because of its natural movement to sink, is used to locate pitches down in the strike zone.

Practice

Pitch the ball using a variety of grips, and see how the ball reacts differently to each pitch. Ask a friend to put on a batting helmet and try to hit a four-seam fastball (right). Move the fingers to the narrow seam for a two-seam fastball.

KNOW THE BATTER

There are dozens of questions that a pitcher can ask about a batter. Knowing more about the batter will help with pitch selection, speed, and the pitcher's overall approach to the game. If the pitcher knows something about each batter, he or she will have more confidence.

If the pitcher knows that a batter stands back in the batter's box more than most players, the pitcher can throw strikes on the outside part of the plate. The batter's bat might not be able to reach those pitches.

If a pitcher sees a batter drop his or her back shoulder, the pitcher can throw high in the strike zone to take advantage of the matchup. A dropped shoulder often means the ball will be hit into the air. High strikes will bring more fly balls.

Practice

When you are pitching to your friends, try to remember the location of pitches they like to hit. Remembering that a certain player likes to hit high pitches, for example, will help you focus on keeping pitches low against him or her.

A catcher is very helpful to a pitcher. He can go to the mound to talk to the pitcher about a batter. The best catchers help calm pitchers and help them stay mentally sharp.

If the coach or manager goes to the mound to visit the same pitcher twice in the same inning, the pitcher must be removed from the game.

Strike Zone

The strike zone is different for everyone. One of the best ways to describe it is the area over home plate between the batter's armpits and knees when the batter is in a position to swing.

FIELDING

Fielding requires great instincts and the ability to make decisions quickly.

Players at each position need to be fast. Infielders need to be able to scoop up the ball with care and know where to throw it after they gather it in. Infielders also need quick reflexes to get to hard-hit balls.

Outfielders must always be aware of their surroundings. How many outs have been made? Where are the base runners? What base should I throw to? Outfielders usually have the strongest arms because they need to be able to throw the ball longer distances than anyone else on the team.

Practice

Just like hitting, fielding is performed best after many repetitions.

Have a teammate throw ground balls to you. Start in the ready position, then move toward the ball after you see if it is going to your left or right. Ask your teammate to throw to different locations.

Step toward the target that you are throwing to in order to make an accurate throw.

When fielding a ball, the main priority is to get directly in front of it with your whole body. Always keep your eyes looking at the target.

Long Toss

Prior to playing a game, young players should start playing catch at a short distance. Toss the ball easily. Then start taking a few steps back after the arm gets warmed up.

Stepping on second base and throwing to first to get the batter out is one way to turn a double play (below).

Bare hand supports glove hand

Eyes should watch the ball all the way into your glove

The center field position requires the most speed in the outfield. Center fielders like Mike Cameron (right) cover a larger territory than other outfielders.

Body pointing toward potential throwing target

Fungo

Warmups at many baseball games include a coach hitting balls to outfielders with a fungo bat. The fungo bat is longer and lighter than bats used in games.

Because the bat is so light, coaches are able to hit balls with accuracy to various spots in the outfield.

No Dives

If the ball is about to land in front of the fielder, it's safer to slide and catch the ball instead of diving head first. The body is under control, and the fielder can watch the ball until it is in the glove.

FIELDING

When the pitcher starts the delivery, the outfielders should get into a ready position and focus on the hitter.

If the fielder does not have to catch the ball on the run, the glove should be brought up to the chest. That way, the glove does not block the view of the ball in the air. Cup the throwing hand under the glove, then cover the opening of the glove as the ball is squeezed into the webbing.

If you will have to make a throw right after catching the ball, take a couple steps back from the spot where the ball will fall. Then move forward as the ball is getting close. Catching the ball on the move will help you have momentum, so your throw will get back to the infield faster.

Which Foot?

If a fly ball is hit to the right side of the outfielder, his or her first step back should be with the right foot. If a fly ball is hit to the outfielder's left side, the first step back should be with the left foot. In each instance, it's the fastest way to get to the ball.

GROUND BALLS

A baseball player needs to concentrate hard in order to cleanly field a ground ball. Prior to the pitch, the fielder should be in the ready position. The fielder's eyes should be on the pitcher. The hands should be out in front of the body in a relaxed position and the feet should be spread shoulder width apart.

When the pitcher starts the delivery, the fielders get into the set position. The fielder's weight should shift to the balls of the feet. The bare hand should be slightly forward of the knee. Be ready to move quickly to either side, up or down.

Bend at the knees and waist, and put the glove all the way down to the ground, open toward the batter. Use the bare hand to cover up the ball after it gets into the glove. Bring both hands to the waist, step and throw.

Practice

Try to catch a ball between hops. Ask a teammate to hit a bouncing ball to you in the infield. Bring your glove up as the ball rises after a bounce, and let the glove act as a cushion for the ball as it rises.

Quick Throws

Shortstops, second basemen, and third basemen are usually right-handed fielders, especially in the major leagues. It's more difficult for a left-handed person to throw the ball to first base quickly from the other infield positions.

In the major leagues, second basemen usually have the smallest gloves on the team. The ball can be handled easier in a small glove.

Use the bare hand to provide balance prior to getting close to the ball

Lean forward and attack the ball

When fielding a ground ball, watch the ball all the way into the glove. Use the bare hand to quickly cover the ball after it gets into the glove. Continue to look at the ball until you have a grip on it with your bare hand. Then focus on the target of your throw.

The glove is open

The ball can't get under the glove →

CATCHER

As the pitcher gets ready to deliver a pitch, the catcher should widen the stance. The bare hand should be made into a fist and placed behind the thumb of the glove. The elbows should be slightly bent.

The catcher should be just far enough behind the batter so the glove arm can be extended with a slight bend in the elbows. The catcher should not be close enough to the plate to interfere with the batter's swing.

Catchers quickly become talented at handling their masks. When a catcher has to make a play on a bunt or short hit, he throws the mask to the side immediately and runs to the ball. On a pop up, the catcher usually holds the mask until he's under the ball. Then he throws the mask out of the way before making the catch.

Practice

On balls down the third base line, pick up the ball with your back toward first base, and then turn and throw. This will help when fielding bunted balls.

FIELDING

Chase any ball that is popped up into foul territory until it goes out of play or hits the ground.

On a bunt, sometimes it's best to hold the ball after you get it in your glove. An errant throw could allow the opposing team's base runners to move around the bases.

If a first or third baseman is able to make a play on a ball, the catcher should let them take it. Players at those positions wear less equipment, so it is easier for them to make a play.

SHORTSTOP

Shortstop is one of the most active fielding positions on the team. Shortstops usually handle more ground balls than any other fielder. They are also responsible for organizing the defense. Shortstops are sometimes called the "quarterback" of the defense.

Shortstop is also one of the most demanding positions. Players who want to play shortstop have to know how to throw and catch. Players also must be agile, because the more reach they have and the faster they get to the ball, the more successful they will be. The shortstop also needs to be a quick thinker. When there are base runners, the shortstop must be able to decide quickly where the ball should be thrown.

A shortstop must be able to dive to the ground in an instant and quickly hop back up to make a throw to first base. Many double plays happen thanks to quick footwork by the shortstop, too.

Coverage

The shortstop is involved any time the ball is hit to the left side of second base. Even if the third baseman handles the ball, the shortstop backs up the play.

Watch the ball
into the glove

Other Duties

Shortstops such as
Derek Jeter cover
second base on balls
hit to the right side
of the field. They
also sometimes
cover second base to
receive a throw from
the catcher when a
base runner is trying
to steal.

Strong,
accurate
arm

Bare hand
cups the ball
into glove

Keep the ball
in the center of
the body

Bend the knees
while catching
the ball

Pivot foot helps to
turn body to target

BASERUNNING

After a batter finds a way to get on base, it's time to get moving on the base paths. Poor baserunning can cost a team runs, and excellent baserunning can be the difference between winning and losing a game.

Baserunning begins the instant the batted ball leaves the bat and is in play. One of the most important points of baserunning is getting out of the batter's box. Batters who are able to drop the bat and sprint to first base quickly will be off to a great start as base runners.

There is no need to slow down as you reach first base. It is the only base you can run past without getting tagged out.

Fast Sprint

A major-league right-handed batter takes an average of 4.3 seconds to run from home plate to first base after making contact with the ball.

For left-handed batters, who are a step closer to the base, the average time is 4.2 seconds. Most high school players run the distance in about 4.5 or 4.6 seconds.

A base runner should drop his or her left shoulder when rounding first, second, or third base. Leaning toward the infield will help create more speed.

Be Aware

Good base runners help their teams score more runs. Being a good base runner takes more than speed, however. Knowing the skills of the players on the other team is important, too. So is keeping track of the situation. By knowing how many outs there are and how well the different fielders can throw and catch, a runner can decide whether to try for an extra base.

Chone Figgins (9) of the Los Angeles Angels of Anaheim stole 41 bases and was thrown out just 12 times in 2007.

RUN TO FIRST BASE

What's the speediest way to get to first base? After you complete the follow through with the bat, drop the bat and begin to make the run to first base. Start out leaning forward slightly. This form will allow for a quicker initial surge out of the batter's box.

Always run with the feet pointing toward first base. Another way to get extra momentum is to pump your arms. Bring your hand all the way up to your chin, and then swing it back around to your back pants pocket. Keep your elbows in near your sides. If your arms move fast, your feet will also move fast. Always run as fast as you can because the first baseman might not catch the throw.

Practice

Ask a teammate to use a stopwatch to time your run from the batter's box to first base. Take a swing, pretend that the ball has been hit, and take off. Be sure to run all the way across first base.

Turn slightly to the right on ground balls thrown by an infielder →

Here are the top eight ways a batter can reach first base:
1. Hit
2. Fielder's Choice
3. Fielder's Error
4. Dropped Third Strike
5. Hit by Pitch
6. Walk
7. Catcher's Interference
8. Runner's Interference (batted ball hits a runner in fair territory. The runner is out, and the batter is awarded a hit).

Face the field when you come to a stop at first base. Base runners can take a look at where the ball is and decide whether to try for second base.

← Run all the way through the base

Use proper balance so that you can run to the left or right

Watch the pitcher

Dive

Dive to the back side of the base. If you do this, the first baseman will have to swipe back farther.

This allows you a fraction of a second more to reach the base than if you dive to the front side of the base.

Knees bent, weight on the balls of the feet

After the pitch leaves the pitcher's glove, shuffle the feet toward second base.

BASERUNNING

By leading off first base, or taking a few steps away from first and moving closer to second base, a base runner is aiming to get to second base faster than a potential throw to that base.

Base runners should always be looking at the pitcher when they take their lead off the base. The safest distance for a lead is one step and a dive. That distance will vary between players.

Leading off can be dangerous. Take too big a lead, and a pitcher can throw out, or pick off, the runner at first.

Maintain your balance while leading off. Leaning too far to second base might allow you to get picked off. Do not start running unless your coach has told you to.

Practice

To determine a safe lead from first base, mark off different distances from first base with your left foot. Dive back to first base to see if you can reach the base on the dive.

Remember the safe distance so that you don't get thrown out.

Once the base runner feels secure in taking the lead from first, stealing second base is a great way to gain an advantage. Every time a runner advances to another base, an opportunity is provided for a batter to drive in a run. Not everyone can hit home runs, but nearly all players are capable of stealing a base.

Make sure that the pitcher is not planning to pick off the runner at first base. When the pitcher has released the ball toward home plate, use the right foot to pivot. Use the left foot to start the momentum toward second base. Stay low and lean forward to build more speed.

As the runner reaches second base, slide into the bag with the right leg extended and the left leg under the right leg.

Practice

Take a lead off first base. Ask a teammate holding a stopwatch on second base to shout, "Go!" and see how fast you can slide into second base. Try to use your momentum to stand up on the base at the end of the slide.

Juan Pierre (9) stole 64 bases in 2007, the second-highest number in the major leagues. He was caught stealing just 15 times. In 2006, he stole 58 bases.

RUNDOWNS

After a base runner commits to advancing to the next base, there's a chance of getting caught in what is called "no-man's land." That is the area of the base path directly between the bases. A rundown occurs when the fielder tries to tag out the base runner before the runner can get close enough to the next base to slide.

Base runners rarely have success in rundowns, but it is possible. Base runners should always look at the ball, never at the fielder. Fielders should always be throwing the ball and running at the same time. If a fielder ever stops throwing, try to get to the base opposite of that fielder.

Practice

Set two teammates equal distances apart on the base path. Stand in between them. Give the ball to one of them and shout, "Go!" Try to get to one base safely before either one of them can apply the tag.

When caught in a rundown between two fielders, be aware that more fielders are coming to help. Fielders back up the two who are involved in the rundown. That way, if the runner gets past one fielder, the ball can simply be thrown to the next fielder. The fielders' goal is to protect the bases, so the runner has no place to go.

Don't Stop

Fielders should always run at the base runner in order to get the runner to stand still. When a runner changes directions, the fielders always get a little bit of an advantage on the runner.

If the fielder holds the ball, sprint in the other direction.

Stay within the base path or it's an automatic out.

Because the runner will be in the base path, fielders should line up about three feet outside the base path. This will prevent the fielder from running into the runner or hitting the runner with the ball. If either of these happen, the runner would be declared safe at the next base by the umpire.

GLOSSARY

★**bunt**—To bat a pitched ball by tapping it lightly so that the ball rolls slowly in front of the infielders.

★**earned-run average**—The average number of earned runs a pitcher gives up per nine innings pitched.

★**fungo**—A fly ball hit for fielding practice by a batter who tosses the ball up and hits it on its way down with a long, thin, light bat.

★**infield**—The area of the field bounded by home plate and first, second, and third bases.

★**momentum**—Force or strength created when running or swinging a bat.

★**outfield**—The area of a baseball playing field beyond the lines connecting the bases.

★**pitcher's mound**—The slight elevation on which the pitcher stands.

★**rundown**—A play in which a runner is trapped between bases and is pursued by fielders attempting to make the tag.

★**sportsmanship**—Good conduct and attitude in sports, including such things as fair play, team spirit, and winning and losing with grace.

★**squeeze play**—A play in which the batter attempts to bunt so that a runner on third base may score.

★**strike zone**—Generally, the area over home plate located between the batter's armpits and knees when the batter is in position to swing the bat.

★**umpire**—The official in charge of a baseball game.

LEARN MORE

INTERNET ADDRESSES

★ **Babe Ruth League Online**
  http://www.baberuthleague.org/

★ **Little League Baseball and Softball Online**
  http://www.littleleague.org

★ **Major League Baseball**
  http://www.mlb.com

★ **Major League Baseball Players Association**
  http://www.mlbplayers.com

★ **PONY Baseball/Softball**
  http://www.pony.org

★ **United States Specialty Sports Association Baseball**
  http://www.usssabaseball.org

BOOKS & VIDEOS

★ **The Art and Science of Hitting .500: In Baseball and Fastpitch Softball at the Highest Levels of Competition,** by Bruce Wright. Charleston, SC: BookSurge Publishing, 2007.

★ **The Baseball Handbook: Winning fundamentals for players and coaches,** By Bernie Walter. Champaign, IL: Human Kinetics, 2002.

★ **The New Authentic Little League Play Ball Training Pack 3 DVD Set,** by Bud Black, Rex Hudler, Dusty Baker, and Reggie Smith. Los Angeles, CA: Peter Pan Studios, 2004.

★ **The Science of Hitting,** by Ted Williams and John Underwood. New York, NY: Simon & Schuster, 1987.

INDEX